Healthy Cooking
MADE EASY

Savor the Flavor

Looking for just the right herb to season your chops, stir into a sauce or toss with pasta? Use the information below to help you make the right choice.

Basil
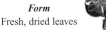

Form
Fresh, dried leaves

Appearance
Fresh basil has oval, silky leaves
with creases.

Flavor
Gives foods a sweet, spicy flavor. Several fresh varieties
are readily available and impart more peppery and robust
flavors.

How to use
Add to meat and poultry dishes, soups, stews and
vegetables. Pairs especially well
with tomatoes.

Sage

Form
Fresh, dried whole, rubbed or ground

Appearance
Fresh sage is characterized by deeply veined,
gray-green leaves.

Flavor
Gives a musty minty taste to foods and
is best known as a seasoning in
poultry stuffings.

How to use
Add to stuffings, sausages, meat loaves, egg dishes, breads
and vegetables. Sage can be used with rosemary, thyme,
oregano and parsley.

Dill

Form
Fresh, dried leaves

Appearance
Fresh dill has tiny, feathery, bright
green leaves.

Flavor
Imparts a light delicate, refreshing taste.

How to use
Toss in salads, add to bread or biscuit dough, fish and
seafood dishes and vegetables.

Paprika

Form
Ground dried mild peppers

Appearance
Red powder

Flavor
This very mild-tasting spice adds more color than
flavor to foods.

How to use
Sprinkle paprika on chicken pieces, pork chops,
fish and egg dishes.

Oregano

Form
Fresh, dried leaves, ground

Appearance
Fresh oregano has small pointed leaves.

Flavor
Bestows a strong spicy flavor with bitter undertones.

How to use
Use oregano to season pork, lamb and poultry. Stir it into
bean soups, tomato sauces, pasta salads, stews and
vegetable dishes.

Thyme

Form
Fresh, dried leaves, ground

Appearance
Fresh thyme has small, oval, grayish leaves.

Flavor
Imparts a heavy, spicy aroma and a pungent clovelike taste.

How to use
Add to chicken, vegetable, fish, meat, meat loaves, egg
dishes and cream sauce. Use with basil or oregano in
tomato mixtures.

Contents

The recipes in Campbell's® Healthy Request™ *Healthy Cooking Made Easy* were developed to help you follow the guidelines of a daily healthy eating plan, which calls for limiting fat to 30% or less of total calories (a maximum of 65g. of fat on a daily 2,000-calorie diet) and limiting sodium to less than 2,400mg. daily. Use the featured menus as a start in developing your own healthy eating plan, and the Food Pyramid as a guide to healthfully rounding out remaining meals, based on recommended daily servings of: 6-11 grain servings, 3-5 vegetable servings, 2-4 fruit servings, 2-3 milk servings and meat servings.

$\mathcal{P}$reparing healthy meals that appeal to you and your family can be easy especially when you have the right ingredients, such as Campbell's® Healthy Request® soups, and meal-planning ideas, such as you'll find in *Healthy Cooking Made Easy*.

$\mathcal{S}$trive for Balance

The key to healthy eating is making sensible food selections. Eat a wide variety of many foods, balancing high-fat, high-calorie and high-sodium foods with those lower in calories, fat and sodium. Round out main dishes of meat, poultry and fish with accompaniments of pasta, rice, dried beans and peas, whole-grain breads and fresh fruits and vegetables.

$\mathcal{M}$ake It a Family Affair

When planning healthy meals, start with foods that you and your family like best. Look for ways to prepare the foods and enhance the flavors without adding unwanted fat, sodium and calories. Choose low-fat cooking methods, such as broiling, grilling, microwaving, roasting, sautéing with nonstick cooking spray and poaching. Lighten up favorite recipes by making ingredient substitutions, replacing ingredients high in fat and sodium with healthier alternatives, such as Campbell's® Healthy Request® soups.

$\mathcal{T}$ry:	$\mathcal{I}$nstead of:
Skillet Herb Roasted Chicken (page 6)	**Traditional roasted chicken**
Creamy Souper Rice (page 80)	**High-sodium packaged rice side dishes**
Broccoli Cheese Potato Topper (page 86)	**Baked potato topped with butter, sour cream and Cheddar cheese**
Healthy Request® Soup or Broth in stir-fries	**High-sodium bouillon**
Healthy Request® Broth to season steamed vegetables	**Butter and salt**

Put Time on Your Side

If you are like most cooks, your best healthy meal intentions are often thwarted by lack of time.

- Try to plan your meals in advance to help keep you from reaching for quick-fix, high-fat, high-salt alternatives when you're facing dinner deadlines.

- Make the most of fresh convenience items, especially pre-cut vegetables and fruits available in the produce section of your supermarket and at the salad bar.

- Keep healthy ingredients on hand, such as bagged frozen vegetables, for ready use. Choose recipes that fit your schedule. Most of the main-dish recipes in *Healthy Cooking Made Easy* can be prepared in less than 30 minutes and are good options for nights when you are pressed for time.

Spice It Up!

Herbs and spices work magic as flavor enhancers and sodium substitutes for healthier cooking. To make the most of them, refer to the chart in the front of this book and these helpful tips:

- Store dried herbs and spices in tightly-covered light-proof containers in a cool, dry place. Replace them annually as they lose flavor over time.

- Crush dried herbs in the palm of your hand, between your fingers, or with a mortar and pestle to release their full flavor potential.

- When substituting a fresh herb for dried, use three times more of the fresh. For example, if a recipe calls for ½ teaspoon dried basil, use 1½ teaspoons of the fresh.

- Store fresh herbs in the refrigerator with their stems in water and cover the leaves with a plastic food storage bag.

- To snip fresh herbs, place the leaves in a custard cup. Use kitchen scissors and short quick strokes to cut the leaves into small pieces.

Focus on Flavor

Easy substitutions and creative cooking ideas can boost flavor and cut unwanted fat, calories and sodium.

- Cook fresh-cut or frozen vegetables in Campbell's® Healthy Request® Chicken Broth to enhance flavor without adding fat.

- Flavor meats, poultry and fish with herbed broth mixtures.

- Replace mild cheeses with more robustly flavored ones and use less. When possible, use reduced-fat varieties.

■ ■ ■ ■ ■ ■ ■ ■ ■ ■ ■ ■ ■ ■

Prep Time: 10 minutes   **Cook Time: 20 minutes**

Skillet Herb Roasted Chicken

¼ teaspoon ground sage
¼ teaspoon dried thyme leaves, crushed
4 skinless, boneless chicken breast halves (about 1 pound)
   Vegetable cooking spray
1 can (10¾ ounces) CAMPBELL'S HEALTHY REQUEST Condensed
   Cream of Chicken Soup
½ cup water
4 cups hot cooked rice, cooked without margarine or salt
   Peach slices for garnish
   Fresh thyme for garnish

1. Mix sage and thyme. Sprinkle chicken with seasoning mixture.

2. Spray medium nonstick skillet with cooking spray and heat over
   medium heat 1 minute. Add chicken and cook 15 minutes or until
   chicken is browned and no longer pink. Remove chicken from skillet
   and keep warm.

3. Add soup and water. Reduce heat to low and heat through. Serve over
   chicken with rice. Garnish with peach slices and fresh thyme. Serves 4.

*In this recipe, Campbell's® Healthy Request® soup substitutes for gravy to create
a rich, delicious dish that's lower in fat and sodium.*

NUTRITIONAL VALUES PER SERVING

Calories	457	Sodium	361mg
Total Fat	5g	Total Carbohydrate	65g
Saturated Fat	2g	Protein	33g
Cholesterol	79mg		

D ad's Turn to Cook

- ≈ *Skillet Herb Roasted Chicken*
- ≈ Steamed green beans
- ≈ Sourdough bread slice with 1 teaspoon margarine
- ≈ ½ cup nonfat frozen yogurt with strawberries

Creamy Chicken & Vegetables

Vegetable cooking spray
4 skinless, boneless chicken breast halves (about 1 pound)
1 can (10¾ ounces) CAMPBELL'S HEALTHY REQUEST
    Condensed Cream of Mushroom Soup
½ cup milk
1 tablespoon lemon juice
¼ teaspoon dried basil leaves, crushed
⅛ teaspoon garlic powder
1 bag (16 ounces) frozen vegetable combination
    (broccoli, cauliflower, carrots)

1. Spray medium skillet with cooking spray and heat over medium-high heat 1 minute. Add chicken and cook 10 minutes or until browned. Set chicken aside.

2. Add soup, milk, lemon juice, basil, garlic powder and vegetables. Heat to a boil. Return chicken to pan. Reduce heat to low. Cover and cook 5 minutes or until chicken is no longer pink. Serves 4.

Serve with rice, cooked in Campbell's® Healthy Request® Ready to Serve Chicken Broth, for a satisfying, healthful accompaniment.

NUTRITIONAL VALUES PER SERVING

Calories	231	Sodium	418mg
Total Fat	5g	Total Carbohydrate	15g
Saturated Fat	2g	Protein	31g
Cholesterol	75mg		

Thirty-Minute Entrées

Savory Lemon Chicken

  Vegetable cooking spray
4 skinless, boneless chicken breast halves (about 1 pound)
1 can (10¾ ounces) CAMPBELL's HEALTHY REQUEST Condensed
   Cream of Chicken Soup
2 tablespoons water
1 tablespoon chopped fresh parsley *or* 1 teaspoon dried parsley flakes
1 tablespoon lemon juice
½ teaspoon paprika
¼ cup chopped green *or* red pepper
  Lemon slices for garnish
  Fresh oregano for garnish

1. Spray medium skillet with cooking spray and heat over medium-high
   heat 1 minute. Add chicken and cook 10 minutes or until browned.
   Set chicken aside.

2. Add soup, water, parsley, lemon juice, paprika and pepper. Heat to a boil.
   Return chicken to pan. Reduce heat to low. Cover and cook 5 minutes or
   until chicken is no longer pink. Garnish with lemon slices and fresh
   oregano. Serves 4.

For the richest depth of flavor, be sure your supply of dried herbs is fresh.
Mark each container with the date of purchase and discard
any remaining herbs after a year.

NUTRITIONAL VALUES PER SERVING

Calories	193	Sodium	360mg
Total Fat	4g	Total Carbohydrate	8g
Saturated Fat	1g	Protein	28g
Cholesterol	79mg		

- *Savory Lemon Chicken*
- Hot cooked pasta cooked without salt
- Steamed carrots
- Small dinner roll with 1 teaspoon margarine
- Fresh strawberries and apples

Chicken in Mushroom Sauce

Vegetable cooking spray
4 skinless, boneless chicken breast halves (about 1 pound)
1 can (10¾ ounces) CAMPBELL'S HEALTHY REQUEST Condensed
     Cream of Mushroom Soup
½ cup milk
4 cups hot cooked corkscrew macaroni (about 3 cups uncooked),
     cooked without salt

1. Spray medium skillet with cooking spray and heat over medium-high
   heat 1 minute. Add chicken and cook 10 minutes or until browned. Set
   chicken aside.

2. Add soup and milk. Heat to a boil. Return chicken to pan. Reduce heat to
   low. Cover and cook 5 minutes or until chicken is no longer pink. Serve
   with macaroni. Serves 4.

*Most grocery stores offer a variety of pasta in many shapes. Corkscrews, bow ties and
wagon wheels are just a few. Corkscrew macaroni is especially nice for this savory dish
because the ridges soak up the creamy sauce, ensuring each
forkful bursts with flavor.*

NUTRITIONAL VALUES PER SERVING

Calories	485	Sodium	379mg
Total Fat	6g	Total Carbohydrate	66g
Saturated Fat	2g	Protein	38g
Cholesterol	75mg		

Thirty-Minute Entrées

Chicken Primavera

1 can (10¾ ounces) CAMPBELL'S HEALTHY REQUEST Condensed
    Cream of Mushroom Soup
½ cup milk
3 tablespoons grated Parmesan cheese
¼ teaspoon garlic powder
1 bag (16 ounces) frozen vegetable combination (broccoli,
    cauliflower, carrots)
2 cups cubed cooked chicken
4 cups hot cooked spaghetti (about 8 ounces uncooked), cooked
    without salt
  Tomatoes for garnish
  Fresh parsley for garnish

1. In medium saucepan mix soup, milk, cheese, garlic powder and
   vegetables. Over medium heat, heat to a boil. Reduce heat to low.
   Cover and cook 10 minutes or until vegetables are tender-crisp,
   stirring occasionally.

2. Stir in chicken and heat through. Serve over spaghetti. Garnish with
   tomatoes and fresh parsley. Serves 4.

*Don't let a shortage of leftover chicken keep you from making this family-pleasing dish.
Just substitute 2 cans (5 ounces each) Swanson® Premium Chunk Chicken Breast,
drained, for the cooked chicken.*

NUTRITIONAL VALUES PER SERVING

Calories	415	Sodium	466mg
Total Fat	9g	Total Carbohydrate	54g
Saturated Fat	3g	Protein	30g
Cholesterol	58mg		

Thirty-Minute Entrées

Skillet Beef 'n' Mac

¾ pound lean ground beef (85% lean)
1 small onion, chopped (about ¼ cup)
½ teaspoon Italian seasoning *or* dried oregano leaves, crushed
1 can (10¾ ounces) CAMPBELL'S HEALTHY REQUEST Condensed
      Tomato Soup
¼ cup water
1 cup frozen whole kernel corn
3 cups cooked corkscrew macaroni (about 2½ cups uncooked), cooked
      without salt
¼ cup grated Parmesan cheese
   Sliced tomatoes for garnish
   Fresh oregano for garnish

1. In medium skillet over medium-high heat, cook beef, onion and Italian
   seasoning until beef is browned, stirring to separate meat. Pour off fat.

2. Add soup, water and corn. Heat to a boil. Reduce heat to low. Cover and
   cook 5 minutes or until corn is tender. Add macaroni and heat through.
   Sprinkle with cheese. Garnish with tomatoes and fresh oregano. Serves 6.

To enjoy the flavor of beef with less fat, be sure to choose ground beef
that is at least 85% lean.

NUTRITIONAL VALUES PER SERVING

Calories	354	Sodium	294mg
Total Fat	9g	Total Carbohydrate	47g
Saturated Fat	3g	Protein	21g
Cholesterol	45mg		

Thirty-Minute Entrées

Chili

¾ pound lean ground beef (85% lean)
1 medium onion, chopped (about ½ cup)
1 tablespoon chili powder
1 can (10¾ ounces) CAMPBELL'S HEALTHY REQUEST
    Condensed Tomato Soup
¼ cup water
1 teaspoon vinegar
1 can (15 ounces) kidney beans, rinsed and drained
4 cups hot cooked rice, cooked without margarine or salt
    Shredded Cheddar cheese for garnish

1. In medium skillet over medium-high heat, cook beef, onion and chili powder until beef is browned, stirring to separate meat. Pour off fat.

2. Add soup, water, vinegar and beans. Heat to a boil. Reduce heat to low. Cook 10 minutes. Serve with rice. Garnish with cheese. Serves 4.

Canned beans score high marks both as health and convenience foods. They are low in fat, rich in fiber, high in protein and easy to use. However, because they contain a lot of sodium, rinse the beans before adding them to the chili to remove excess sodium.

NUTRITIONAL VALUES PER SERVING

Calories	555	Sodium	576mg
Total Fat	12g	Total Carbohydrate	81g
Saturated Fat	4g	Protein	29g
Cholesterol	63mg		

Halftime Buffet

- ∼ *Chili*
- ∼ Fat-free tortilla chips with salsa
- ∼ Fat-free corn muffins
- ∼ Spinach salad with mushrooms and fat-free dressing

Spicy Cheese Twisters

**1 can (10¾ ounces) CAMPBELL'S HEALTHY REQUEST Condensed
    Cream of Chicken Soup**
½ cup skim milk
**⅓ cup cubed pasteurized process cheese spread
    with jalapeño pepper (3 ounces)**
**3 cups hot cooked corkscrew macaroni (about 2½ cups uncooked),
    cooked without salt**
  Chopped fresh parsley for garnish

In medium saucepan mix soup, milk and cheese. Over low heat, heat until cheese is melted, stirring often. Toss with macaroni. Garnish with fresh parsley. Serves 4.

Microwave Directions

In microwave-safe bowl mix soup, milk and cheese. Cover and microwave on HIGH 3 minutes. Stir. Cover and microwave on HIGH 3 minutes or until cheese is melted. Stir. Toss with macaroni.

Instead of traditional Macaroni and Cheese, try Spicy Cheese Twisters with only 6 grams of total fat per serving. If spicy-hot dishes fail to suit your fancy, substitute plain pasteurized process cheese for the jalapeño cheese spread.

NUTRITIONAL VALUES PER SERVING

Calories	268	Sodium	635mg
Total Fat	6g	Total Carbohydrate	41g
Saturated Fat	4g	Protein	11g
Cholesterol	22mg		

Thirty-Minute Entrées

 Easy Skillet Pork Chops

Vegetable cooking spray
4 pork chops, ¾ inch thick (about 1½ pounds)
1 can (10¾ ounces) CAMPBELL'S HEALTHY REQUEST Condensed
    Cream of Celery Soup
¼ cup apple juice *or* water
2 tablespoons spicy-brown mustard
1 tablespoon honey
⅛ teaspoon pepper
4 cups hot cooked cholesterol-free noodle-style pasta (about 4 cups
    uncooked), cooked without salt
Fresh parsley for garnish

1. Spray medium skillet with cooking spray and heat over medium-high
   heat 1 minute. Add chops and cook 10 minutes or until browned. Set
   chops aside.

2. Add soup, apple juice, mustard, honey and pepper. Heat to a boil. Return
   chops to pan. Reduce heat to low. Cover and cook 10 minutes or until
   chops are no longer pink. Serve with pasta. Garnish with fresh parsley.
   Serves 4.

For extra flavor and a spark of color, toss hot cooked noodles with chopped fresh herbs.
Mild tasting herbs, such as parsley, pair well with any dish. Or experiment with a stronger
herb, such as oregano or basil.

NUTRITIONAL VALUES PER SERVING

Calories	438	Sodium	534mg
Total Fat	10g	Total Carbohydrate	51g
Saturated Fat	3g	Protein	31g
Cholesterol	70mg		

Thirty-Minute Entrées

Prep Time: 20 minutes   **Cook Time: 20 minutes**

Chicken & Vegetable Stir-Fry

2 tablespoons cornstarch
1 can (16 ounces) CAMPBELL'S HEALTHY REQUEST Ready to Serve Chicken Broth
Vegetable cooking spray
1 pound skinless, boneless chicken breasts, cut into strips
2 teaspoons low-sodium soy sauce
5 cups cut-up vegetables*
4 cups hot cooked rice, cooked without margarine or salt

1. In cup mix cornstarch and *½ cup* broth until smooth. Set aside.

2. Spray medium skillet with cooking spray and heat over medium-high heat 1 minute. Add chicken in 2 batches and stir-fry until browned. Set chicken aside.

3. Add remaining broth, soy and vegetables. Heat to a boil. Reduce heat to low. Cover and cook 5 minutes or until vegetables are tender-crisp.

4. Stir cornstarch mixture and add. Cook until mixture boils and thickens, stirring constantly. Return chicken to pan and heat through. Serve over rice. Serves 4.

* **Use a combination of broccoli flowerets, sliced carrots and green *or* red pepper strips.**

NUTRITIONAL VALUES PER SERVING

Calories	472	Sodium	394mg
Total Fat	4g	Total Carbohydrate	71g
Saturated Fat	1g	Protein	36g
Cholesterol	72mg		

*E*asy Lemon Broccoli Chicken

Vegetable cooking spray
1 pound skinless, boneless chicken breasts, cut into strips
1 can (10¼ ounces) CAMPBELL'S HEALTHY REQUEST Condensed
  Cream of Broccoli Soup
½ cup milk
1 tablespoon lemon juice
⅛ teaspoon garlic powder
⅛ teaspoon pepper
2 cups cooked broccoli flowerets
4 cups hot cooked rice, cooked without margarine or salt
Lemon slices for garnish
Red onion wedges for garnish

1. Spray medium skillet with cooking spray and heat over medium-high heat
   1 minute. Add chicken in 2 batches and cook until browned, stirring
   often. Set chicken aside.

2. Add soup, milk, lemon juice, garlic powder, pepper and broccoli. Heat to
   a boil. Return chicken to pan and heat through. Serve over rice. Garnish
   with lemon and red onion. Serves 4.

*When cooking rice or pasta, to add flavor without adding fat, substitute Campbell's®
Healthy Request® Ready to Serve Chicken Broth for traditional water and butter or oil.*

NUTRITIONAL VALUES PER SERVING

Calories	488	Sodium	396mg
Total Fat	8g	Total Carbohydrate	69g
Saturated Fat	3g	Protein	31g
Cholesterol	69mg		

Souper One-Dish Suppers

Savory Chicken & Rice

Vegetable cooking spray
2 cups broccoli flowerets
2 cups sliced mushrooms (about 6 ounces)
1 pound skinless, boneless chicken breasts, cut up
**1 can (10¾ ounces) CAMPBELL'S HEALTHY REQUEST Condensed
    Cream of Chicken & Broccoli Soup**
¼ cup milk
¼ cup Chablis *or* other dry white wine
1 tablespoon Dijon-style mustard
4 cups hot cooked rice, cooked without margarine or salt
Tomato wedges for garnish
Fresh sage for garnish

1. Spray medium skillet with cooking spray and heat over medium heat
   1 minute. Add broccoli and mushrooms and cook until tender-crisp.
   Set vegetables aside.

2. Remove pan from heat. Spray with cooking spray. Increase heat to
   medium-high. Add chicken and cook until browned, stirring often.
   Set chicken aside.

3. Add soup, milk, wine and mustard. Heat to a boil. Return vegetables and
   chicken to pan. Reduce heat to low. Cover and cook 5 minutes or until
   chicken is no longer pink. Serve over rice. Garnish with tomato wedges
   and fresh sage. Serves 4.

*A little wine lends an elegant touch to this simple dish. If you prefer
a nonalcoholic version that tastes equally delicious, omit
the wine and increase the milk to one-half cup.*

NUTRITIONAL VALUES PER SERVING

Calories	501	Sodium	472mg
Total Fat	6g	Total Carbohydrate	69g
Saturated Fat	2g	Protein	37g
Cholesterol	77mg		

Souper One-Dish Suppers

 Chicken Tetrazzini with a Twist

3 cups uncooked corkscrew macaroni
1 medium zucchini, shredded (about 1¼ cups)
1 medium carrot, shredded (about ½ cup)
1 tablespoon olive oil
1 small onion, chopped (about ¼ cup)
1 can (10¾ ounces) CAMPBELL'S HEALTHY REQUEST Condensed
    Cream of Mushroom Soup
¼ cup milk
¼ cup low-fat sour cream
1 tablespoon grated Parmesan cheese
2 cans (5 ounces *each*) SWANSON Premium Chunk Chicken Breast *or*
    Chunk Chicken, drained
    Carrot curls for garnish
    Fresh oregano for garnish

1. In large saucepan prepare macaroni according to package directions, omit-
   ting salt. Add zucchini and carrot for last 1 minute of cooking time. Drain
   in colander.

2. In same pan over medium heat, heat oil. Add onion and cook until tender.
   Add soup, milk, sour cream, cheese, chicken and macaroni mixture. Heat
   through, stirring occasionally. Garnish with carrot curls and fresh oregano.
   Serves 4.

*Olive oil is a monounsaturated fat that is often a preferred substitute for saturated fat
and other oils. But keep in mind that all fats, including olive oil, should be used only
in moderation. In this dish, a small amount flavors the sauce
without breaking your fat budget.*

NUTRITIONAL VALUES PER SERVING

Calories	477	Sodium	569mg
Total Fat	10g	Total Carbohydrate	70g
Saturated Fat	3g	Protein	27g
Cholesterol	38mg		

Souper   One-Dish   Suppers

 Creamy Chicken Stir-Fry

Vegetable cooking spray
3 cups cut-up vegetables*
1 pound skinless, boneless chicken breasts, cut into strips
1 can (10¾ ounces) CAMPBELL'S HEALTHY REQUEST Condensed
    Cream of Celery Soup
½ cup milk
1 tablespoon low-sodium soy sauce
¼ teaspoon garlic powder
4 cups hot cooked rice, cooked without margarine or salt

1. Spray medium skillet with cooking spray and heat over medium heat 1 minute. Add vegetables and stir-fry until tender-crisp. Set vegetables aside.

2. Remove pan from heat. Spray with cooking spray. Increase heat to medium-high. Add chicken in 2 batches and stir-fry until browned. Set chicken aside.

3. Add soup, milk, soy and garlic powder. Heat to a boil. Return vegetables and chicken to pan and heat through. Serve over rice. Serves 4.

* Use a combination of broccoli flowerets, sliced carrots and green *or* red pepper strips.

Broccoli and cauliflower are excellent sources of vitamin C, while carrots provide beta carotene, an important antioxidant. Include these vegetables in your meals regularly, as part of a naturally well-balanced diet.

NUTRITIONAL VALUES PER SERVING

Calories	494	Sodium	517mg
Total Fat	6g	Total Carbohydrate	72g
Saturated Fat	2g	Protein	35g
Cholesterol	78mg		

Souper One-Dish Suppers

Stroganoff-Style Chicken

Vegetable cooking spray
1 pound skinless, boneless chicken breasts, cut into strips
2 cups sliced mushrooms (about 6 ounces)
1 medium onion, chopped (about ½ cup)
**1 can (10¾ ounces) CAMPBELL'S HEALTHY REQUEST Condensed
   Cream of Chicken Soup**
½ cup plain nonfat yogurt
¼ cup water
**4 cups hot cooked cholesterol-free noodle-style pasta (about 4 cups
     uncooked), cooked without salt**
Paprika
Fresh parsley for garnish

1. Spray medium nonstick skillet with cooking spray and heat over medium-high heat 1 minute. Add chicken in 2 batches and cook until browned, stirring often. Set chicken aside.

2. Remove pan from heat. Spray with cooking spray. Add mushrooms and onion and cook until tender.

3. Add soup, yogurt and water. Heat to a boil. Return chicken to pan and heat through. Garnish pasta with chopped fresh parsley. Serve over pasta. Sprinkle with paprika. Serves 4.

This recipe substitutes Campbell's® Healthy Request® Condensed Cream of Chicken Soup for the high-fat sour cream in traditional Stroganoff to bring you a deliciously healthier version of the classic.

NUTRITIONAL VALUES PER SERVING

Calories	421	Sodium	384mg
Total Fat	5g	Total Carbohydrate	53g
Saturated Fat	2g	Protein	37g
Cholesterol	79mg		

Chicken Broccoli Vegetable Sauté

Vegetable cooking spray
4 skinless, boneless chicken breast halves (about 1 pound)
1 can (10¾ ounces) CAMPBELL'S HEALTHY REQUEST Condensed
 Cream of Broccoli Soup
½ cup milk
¼ teaspoon dried basil leaves, crushed
⅛ teaspoon pepper
1 bag (16 ounces) frozen vegetable combination (broccoli,
 cauliflower, carrots)

1. Spray medium skillet with cooking spray and heat over medium-high
   heat 1 minute. Add chicken and cook 10 minutes or until browned. Set
   chicken aside.

2. Add soup, milk, basil, pepper and vegetables. Heat to a boil. Return chicken
   to pan. Reduce heat to low. Cover and cook 5 minutes or until chicken is no
   longer pink. Serves 4.

Frozen packaged vegetable combinations perk up meals by adding
color and variety—open just one package and you have
three or more kinds of vegetables ready to use.

NUTRITIONAL VALUES PER SERVING

Calories	229	Sodium	395mg
Total Fat	5g	Total Carbohydrate	13g
Saturated Fat	2g	Protein	32g
Cholesterol	78mg		

Southwest Chicken & Vegetables

Vegetable cooking spray
4 skinless, boneless chicken breast halves (about 1 pound)
1 can (10¼ ounces) CAMPBELL'S HEALTHY REQUEST Condensed
    Cream of Chicken & Broccoli Soup
½ cup milk
2 tablespoons lime *or* lemon juice
1 tablespoon chopped fresh cilantro *or* parsley
⅛ teaspoon pepper
3 cups cut-up vegetables*
4 cups hot cooked rice, cooked without margarine or salt
Lime slices for garnish
Curly endive for garnish

1. Spray medium skillet with cooking spray and heat over medium-high heat 1 minute. Add chicken and cook 10 minutes or until browned. Set chicken aside.

2. Add soup, milk, lime juice, cilantro, pepper and vegetables. Heat to a boil. Return chicken to pan. Reduce heat to low. Cover and cook 5 minutes or until chicken is no longer pink. Serve with rice. Serve with additional lime juice if desired. Garnish with lime slices and curly endive. Serves 4.

* Use a combination of broccoli flowerets, whole kernel corn and green *or* red pepper strips.

Pungent cilantro evokes strong opinions—you either love it or prefer to leave it. If you are among the latter, opt for parsley as an ingredient.

NUTRITIONAL VALUES PER SERVING

Calories	503	Sodium	385mg
Total Fat	6g	Total Carbohydrate	73g
Saturated Fat	2g	Protein	37g
Cholesterol	78mg		

S o u p e r   O n e - D i s h   S u p p e r s

omato Chicken Stir-Fry

Vegetable cooking spray
3 cups cut-up vegetables*
¼ teaspoon garlic powder *or* 2 cloves garlic, minced
1 pound skinless, boneless chicken breasts, cut into strips
1 can (10¾ ounces) CAMPBELL'S HEALTHY REQUEST Condensed Tomato Soup
1 tablespoon vinegar
2 teaspoons low-sodium soy sauce
⅛ teaspoon hot pepper sauce
2 packages (2.8 ounces *each*) CAMPBELL'S Baked Chicken Flavor Ramen Noodle Soup

1. Spray medium skillet with cooking spray. Heat over medium heat 1 minute. Add vegetables and garlic powder and stir-fry until tender-crisp. Set vegetables aside.

2. Remove pan from heat. Spray with cooking spray. Increase heat to medium-high. Add chicken in 2 batches and stir-fry until browned. Set chicken aside.

3. Add soup, vinegar, soy and hot pepper sauce. Heat to a boil. Return vegetables and chicken to pan and heat through.

4. Cook noodles according to package directions. (Reserve seasoning packets for another use.) Drain. Serve chicken mixture over noodles. Serves 4.

* **Use a combination of broccoli flowerets, carrots cut into matchstick-thin strips and green *or* red pepper strips.**

NUTRITIONAL VALUES PER SERVING

Calories	358	Sodium	606mg
Total Fat	5g	Total Carbohydrate	48g
Saturated Fat	1g	Protein	32g
Cholesterol	72mg		

Beef & Mushrooms Dijon

¾ pound boneless beef sirloin steak *or* top round steak, ¾ inch thick
    Vegetable cooking spray
2 cups sliced mushrooms (about 6 ounces)
1 medium onion, sliced (about ½ cup)
1 can (10¾ ounces) CAMPBELL'S HEALTHY REQUEST Condensed
    Cream of Mushroom Soup
¼ cup water
2 tablespoons Dijon-style mustard
4 cups hot cooked rice, cooked without margarine or salt
    Lemon peel for garnish
    Fresh sage for garnish

1. Slice beef into very thin strips. Set beef aside.

2. Spray medium skillet with cooking spray and heat over medium heat 1 minute. Add mushrooms and onion and cook until tender. Set vegetables aside.

3. Remove pan from heat. Spray with cooking spray. Increase heat to medium-high. Add beef and cook until browned, stirring often.

4. Add soup, water and mustard. Heat to a boil. Return vegetables to pan and heat through. Serve over rice. Garnish with lemon peel and fresh sage. Serves 4.

Mushrooms bestow an earthy flavor and meaty texture to many dishes while barely raising the calorie count. For the best texture and flavor, clean mushrooms by wiping them with a damp cloth.

NUTRITIONAL VALUES PER SERVING

Calories	452	Sodium	522mg
Total Fat	7g	Total Carbohydrate	67g
Saturated Fat	3g	Protein	27g
Cholesterol	57mg		

Souper One-Dish Suppers

riental Beef & Vegetable Skillet

1 pound boneless beef sirloin steak *or* top round steak, ¾ inch thick
    Vegetable cooking spray
2 cups broccoli flowerets
2 cups sliced mushrooms (about 6 ounces)
2 medium onions, cut into wedges
1 can (10¾ ounces) CAMPBELL'S HEALTHY REQUEST Condensed
       Cream of Mushroom Soup
½ cup water
1 tablespoon low-sodium soy sauce
¼ teaspoon garlic powder *or* 2 cloves garlic, minced
4 cups hot cooked rice, cooked without margarine or salt
    Chopped red pepper for garnish

1. Slice beef into very thin strips. Set beef aside.

2. Spray medium skillet with cooking spray and heat over medium heat
   1 minute. Add broccoli, mushrooms and onions and cook until tender-crisp.
   Set vegetables aside.

3. Remove pan from heat. Spray with cooking spray. Increase heat to medium-
   high. Add beef in 2 batches and cook until browned, stirring often. Set aside.

4. Add soup, water, soy and garlic powder. Heat to a boil. Return vegetables
   and beef to pan and heat through. Toss rice with chopped red pepper. Serve
   over rice. Serves 4.

You can make beef part of your healthy diet as long as you choose lean cuts. Look for cuts
from the loin, such as tenderloin and sirloin, or round cuts, such as top or bottom
round and eye of round.

NUTRITIONAL VALUES PER SERVING

Calories	587	Sodium	494mg
Total Fat	16g	Total Carbohydrate	76g
Saturated Fat	6g	Protein	34g
Cholesterol	79mg		

Creative Chef™ **Pasta Primavera**

1 can (10¾ ounces) CAMPBELL'S HEALTHY REQUEST *Creative Chef*™
   Condensed Cream of Mushroom with Roasted Garlic & Herbs Soup
½ cup milk
3 tablespoons grated Parmesan cheese
1 tablespoon lemon juice
⅛ teaspoon pepper
3 cups cut-up vegetables*
2 cups hot cooked spaghetti (about 4 ounces uncooked), cooked
   without salt

1. In medium skillet mix soup, milk, cheese, lemon juice and pepper. Over medium heat, heat to a boil.

2. Add vegetables. Reduce heat to low. Cover and cook 15 minutes or until vegetables are tender, stirring occasionally. Toss with spaghetti. Serves 4.

* Use a combination of broccoli flowerets, cauliflower flowerets and green *or* red pepper strips.

Parmesan cheese packs a lot of flavor in a small amount and presents a healthier alternative to butter or oil to flavor pasta, potatoes and salad.

NUTRITIONAL VALUES PER SERVING

Calories	194	Sodium	396mg
Total Fat	4g	Total Carbohydrate	32g
Saturated Fat	2g	Protein	8g
Cholesterol	8mg		

𝒫asta Dinner

~ *Creative Chef™ Pasta Primavera*

~ Italian bread slice with 1 teaspoon margarine

~ ½ cup fat-free sorbet

Spaghetti Florentine

Vegetable cooking spray
1 medium onion, chopped (about ½ cup)
3 cloves garlic, minced
1 teaspoon Italian seasoning, crushed
1 can (10¾ ounces) CAMPBELL'S HEALTHY REQUEST
    Condensed Cream of Celery Soup
⅛ teaspoon pepper
1 package (about 10 ounces) frozen chopped spinach
1 cup plain nonfat yogurt
1 medium tomato, diced (about 1 cup)
4 cups hot cooked spaghetti (about 8 ounces uncooked), cooked
    without salt
2 tablespoons grated Parmesan cheese
Sliced tomatoes for garnish
Fresh oregano for garnish

1. Spray medium saucepan with cooking spray and heat over medium heat 1 minute. Add onion, garlic and Italian seasoning and cook until tender.

2. Add soup, pepper and spinach. Heat to a boil. Reduce heat to low. Cover and cook 10 minutes or until spinach is tender, breaking apart spinach with fork and stirring occasionally.

3. Add yogurt and tomato and heat through. Toss with spaghetti. Sprinkle with cheese. Garnish with tomato and fresh oregano. Serves 4.

Eating meatless meals now and then makes good health sense. This pasta dish serves four as a hearty no-meat entrée or six as a delicious side to baked fish or oven-roasted poultry.

NUTRITIONAL VALUES PER SERVING

Calories	322	Sodium	444mg
Total Fat	3g	Total Carbohydrate	59g
Saturated Fat	1g	Protein	14g
Cholesterol	6mg		

S o u p e r   O n e - D i s h   S u p p e r s

Prep Time: 10 minutes   **Cook Time: 30 minutes**

erbed Chicken & Rice

1 can (10¾ ounces) CAMPBELL'S HEALTHY REQUEST Condensed
    Cream of Mushroom Soup
1¼ cups water
½ teaspoon dried thyme *or* rosemary leaves, crushed
⅛ teaspoon pepper
1 cup uncooked quick-cooking brown rice
4 skinless, boneless chicken breast halves (about 1 pound)
    Paprika
    Fresh thyme for garnish

1. In 2-quart shallow baking dish mix soup, water, thyme, pepper and rice. Arrange chicken on rice mixture. Sprinkle chicken with paprika.

2. Bake at 400°F. for 30 minutes or until chicken is no longer pink and rice is done. Garnish with fresh thyme. Serves 4.

Brown rice makes a nice change of pace from the more familiar white rice. While enjoying its rich nutty flavor and chewy texture, you will also increase the fiber in your diet.

NUTRITIONAL VALUES PER SERVING

Calories	349	Sodium	362mg
Total Fat	6g	Total Carbohydrate	42g
Saturated Fat	2g	Protein	31g
Cholesterol	72mg		

Chicken Broccoli Divan

1 **pound broccoli trimmed, cut into 2-inch pieces (about 4 cups), cooked and drained**
2 **cans (5 ounces *each*) SWANSON Premium Chunk Chicken Breast, drained**
1 **can (10¾ ounces) CAMPBELL'S HEALTHY REQUEST Condensed Cream of Chicken Soup**
½ **cup milk**
⅛ **teaspoon pepper**
¼ **cup shredded reduced-fat Cheddar cheese (1 ounce)
   Halved cherry tomatoes for garnish**

1. In 2-quart shallow baking dish arrange broccoli and chicken. In small bowl mix soup, milk and pepper and pour over broccoli and chicken.

2. Sprinkle cheese over soup mixture. Bake at 450°F. for 15 minutes or until hot. Garnish with tomatoes. Serves 4.

If you're forever searching for supper ideas that require no last-minute shopping trips, try this easy casserole. Keep frozen broccoli in the freezer and substitute it for fresh. Cook and drain 1 bag (about 16 ounces) frozen broccoli cuts and place in the casserole with the chicken. Continue as directed in the recipe.

NUTRITIONAL VALUES PER SERVING

Calories	192	Sodium	624mg
Total Fat	4g	Total Carbohydrate	15g
Saturated Fat	3g	Protein	23g
Cholesterol	51mg		

 Chicken Mozzarella

4 skinless, boneless chicken breast halves (about 1 pound)
1 can (10¾ ounces) CAMPBELL'S HEALTHY REQUEST Condensed
        Tomato Soup
½ teaspoon Italian seasoning *or* dried oregano leaves, crushed
½ teaspoon garlic powder
¼ cup shredded mozzarella cheese (1 ounce)
4 cups hot cooked corkscrew macaroni (about 3 cups uncooked),
        cooked without salt
   Fresh basil for garnish

1. Place chicken in 2-quart shallow baking dish. Mix soup, Italian seasoning and garlic powder. Spoon over chicken and bake at 400°F. for 20 minutes or until chicken is no longer pink.

2. Sprinkle cheese over chicken. Remove chicken. Stir sauce. Serve with macaroni. Garnish with fresh basil. Serves 4.

To make the most of your cooking time, start by heating the water for the macaroni.
While the chicken bakes, you can cook the macaroni.

NUTRITIONAL VALUES PER SERVING

Calories	559	Sodium	385mg
Total Fat	7g	Total Carbohydrate	80g
Saturated Fat	2g	Protein	41g
Cholesterol	78mg		

E a s y   O v e n   D i n n e r s

$\mathcal{L}$emon Thyme Chicken Crunch

1 can (10¾ ounces) CAMPBELL'S HEALTHY REQUEST Condensed Cream of Chicken Soup
¼ cup water
1 tablespoon lemon juice
⅛ teaspoon dried thyme *or* basil leaves, crushed
⅔ cup dry bread crumbs
¼ teaspoon paprika
4 chicken breast halves (about 2 pounds), skinned
Vegetable cooking spray (optional)
Lemon slices for garnish

1. In small saucepan mix soup, water, lemon juice and thyme.

2. Mix bread crumbs and paprika on plate. Dip chicken into *½ cup* soup mixture. Coat with bread crumb mixture.

3. Place chicken on baking sheet. Spray chicken with cooking spray if desired. Bake at 375°F. for 1 hour or until chicken is no longer pink.

4. Heat remaining soup mixture. Serve with chicken. Garnish with lemon slices. Serves 4.

For an elegant meal, pair this piquant chicken with linguine tossed with chopped red pepper and fresh parsley. Add a savory side of sugar snap peas cooked in a small amount of Campbell's® Healthy Request® Ready to Serve Chicken Broth.

NUTRITIONAL VALUES PER SERVING

Calories	263	Sodium	515mg
Total Fat	5g	Total Carbohydrate	21g
Saturated Fat	2g	Protein	30g
Cholesterol	79mg		

E a s y   O v e n   D i n n e r s

Marinated Orange Chicken & Vegetables

¼ cup orange juice
½ teaspoon dried thyme leaves *or* ¼ teaspoon dried rosemary
    leaves, crushed
  Generous dash pepper
4 skinless, boneless chicken breast halves (about 1 pound)
1 can (10¾ ounces) CAMPBELL'S HEALTHY REQUEST Condensed
    Cream of Chicken Soup
2 large carrots, cut into 2-inch matchstick-thin strips (about 2 cups)
1 medium zucchini, sliced (about 2 cups)
4 orange slices for garnish
  Fresh rosemary for garnish

1. Mix orange juice, thyme and pepper in 2-quart shallow baking dish.
   Add chicken and turn to coat. Cover and refrigerate 30 minutes, turning
   chicken occasionally. Spoon off marinade and reserve.

2. Mix soup, carrots, zucchini and reserved marinade. Pour over chicken.

3. Cover. Bake at 400°F. for 30 minutes or until chicken is no longer pink.
   Remove chicken. Stir sauce. Serve with chicken. Garnish with orange
   slices and fresh rosemary. Serves 4.

*A sauce of Campbell's® Healthy Request® soup, juice and herbs moisturizes and flavors the
chicken for a healthier alternative to a traditional marinade high in fat and sodium.*

NUTRITIONAL VALUES PER SERVING

Calories	259	Sodium	383mg
Total Fat	5g	Total Carbohydrate	23g
Saturated Fat	2g	Protein	30g
Cholesterol	79mg		

Easy Oven Dinners

roccoli Fish Bake

1 package (about 10 ounces) frozen broccoli spears, cooked and
   drained *or* 1 pound fresh broccoli, cut into spears, cooked
   and drained
1 pound fresh *or* thawed frozen firm white fish fillets
1 can (10¼ ounces) CAMPBELL'S HEALTHY REQUEST Condensed
   Cream of Broccoli Soup
⅓ cup milk
¼ cup shredded Cheddar cheese (1 ounce)
2 tablespoons dry bread crumbs
1 teaspoon margarine, melted
⅛ teaspoon paprika
   Lemon slices for garnish
   Fresh dill for garnish

1. In 2-quart shallow baking dish arrange broccoli. Top with fish. In small
   bowl mix soup and milk and pour over fish.

2. Sprinkle cheese over soup mixture. Mix bread crumbs, margarine and
   paprika and sprinkle over cheese. Bake at 450°F. for 20 minutes or until
   fish flakes easily when tested with a fork. Garnish with lemon and fresh
   dill. Serves 4.

*Different kinds of fish have different flavors and textures. For this casserole, choose a fish
with a delicate flavor and firm texture, such as cod, haddock or halibut.*

NUTRITIONAL VALUES PER SERVING

Calories	214	Sodium	472mg
Total Fat	6g	Total Carbohydrate	12g
Saturated Fat	3g	Protein	26g
Cholesterol	60mg		

𝓔asy & Lite Dinner

- ∽ *Broccoli Fish Bake*
- ∽ **Brown rice cooked without margarine or salt**
- ∽ **French bread slice with 1 teaspoon margarine**
- ∽ **Fresh strawberries with fat-free whipped topping**

Sumptuous Soups

Prep Time: 15 minutes   **Cook Time: 25 minutes**

Mexican Chicken Soup

Vegetable cooking spray
1 pound skinless, boneless chicken breasts, cut into cubes
1 large green *or* red pepper, coarsely chopped (about 1 cup)
2 teaspoons chili powder
1 teaspoon garlic powder
2 cans (16 ounces *each*) CAMPBELL'S HEALTHY REQUEST
    Ready to Serve Chicken Broth
1 package (10 ounces) frozen whole kernel corn
    (about 1¾ cups)
1 cup cooked rice, cooked without margarine or salt
1 teaspoon chopped fresh cilantro *or* parsley (optional)
5 lime wedges
    Fresh cilantro sprigs for garnish

1. Spray large saucepan with cooking spray and heat over medium heat
   1 minute. Add chicken, pepper, chili powder and garlic powder. Cook
   5 minutes, stirring often.

2. Add broth, corn and rice. Heat to a boil. Reduce heat to low. Cook
   10 minutes or until chicken is no longer pink. Stir in cilantro. Serve with
   lime wedges and garnish with fresh cilantro sprigs. Serves 5.

*With the popularity of Mexican foods, chili powder has moved to the front of the spice
cabinet. Cooking the chili powder with the chicken enriches and mellows its spicy flavor.*

NUTRITIONAL VALUES PER SERVING

Calories	243	Sodium	419mg
Total Fat	3g	Total Carbohydrate	27g
Saturated Fat	1g	Protein	27g
Cholesterol	58mg		

*M*ac 'n' Beef Soup

½ **pound lean ground beef (85% lean)**
1 **medium onion, chopped (about ½ cup)**
1 **small green pepper, chopped (about ½ cup)**
½ **teaspoon dried basil leaves, crushed**
½ **teaspoon dried oregano leaves, crushed**
3 **cans (10¾ ounces *each*) CAMPBELL'S HEALTHY REQUEST**
    Condensed Tomato Soup
4 **cups water**
2 **teaspoons lemon juice**
4 **cups cooked elbow macaroni (about 2 cups uncooked), cooked**
    without salt

1. In large saucepan over medium-high heat, cook beef, onion, pepper, basil and oregano until beef is browned, stirring to separate meat. Pour off fat.

2. Add soup, water, lemon juice and macaroni. Reduce heat to low and heat through. Serves 8.

Count on green peppers to add a spark of color and fresh flavor to soups, salads and main dishes. When purchasing green peppers, look for ones that are glossy, firm and well-shaped. Avoid those with soft spots and blemishes.

NUTRITIONAL VALUES PER SERVING

Calories	255	Sodium	448mg
Total Fat	5g	Total Carbohydrate	41g
Saturated Fat	1g	Protein	12g
Cholesterol	21mg		

Sunday Afternoon Lunch

≈ *Mac 'n' Beef Soup*

≈ Sesame bread sticks

≈ Tossed green salad with fat-free dressing

≈ Medium sliced apple

≈ ½ cup sugar-free pudding

 earty Tomato Rice Soup

Vegetable cooking spray
1 small zucchini, coarsely chopped (about 1 cup)
½ teaspoon dried basil leaves, crushed
⅛ teaspoon garlic powder *or* 1 clove garlic, minced
1 can (10¾ ounces) CAMPBELL'S HEALTHY REQUEST Condensed
   Tomato Soup
1⅓ cups water
1 teaspoon lemon juice
1½ cups cooked rice, cooked without margarine or salt
2 tablespoons grated Parmesan cheese

1. Spray medium saucepan with cooking spray and heat over medium heat 1 minute. Add zucchini, basil and garlic powder and cook until tender-crisp.

2. Add soup, water, lemon juice and rice. Heat through. Sprinkle with cheese. Serves 4.

Paired with a salad or sandwich, this soup fits the bill for lunch at school or office. Transport the soup in an insulated vacuum bottle, or keep it chilled until lunch time and reheat in a microwave oven.

NUTRITIONAL VALUES PER SERVING

Calories	162	Sodium	334mg
Total Fat	2g	Total Carbohydrate	32g
Saturated Fat	1g	Protein	5g
Cholesterol	3mg		

Prep Time: 15 minutes   **Cook Time: 10 minutes**

Vegetable Tortilla Triangles

1 can (10¾ ounces) **CAMPBELL'S HEALTHY REQUEST** Condensed
     Cream of Celery Soup
1 medium tomato, chopped (about 1 cup)
1 small green pepper, chopped (about ½ cup)
2 green onions, sliced (about ¼ cup)
1 jalapeño pepper, seeded and finely chopped (about 1 tablespoon)
     (optional)
8 flour tortillas (8-inch)
1 cup shredded Cheddar cheese (4 ounces)
     Chili peppers for garnish
     Fresh cilantro for garnish

1. Mix soup, tomato, green pepper, onions and jalapeño pepper.

2. Place tortillas on 2 baking sheets. Top each tortilla with ⅓ cup soup mixture. Spread to within ½ inch of edge. Top with cheese.

3. Bake at 400°F. for 10 minutes or until tortillas are crisp. Cut each into quarters. Garnish with chili peppers and fresh cilantro. Makes 32 appetizers.

Jalapeño peppers contain oils that can burn your eyes, lips and skin. Protect yourself by wearing plastic gloves on your hands when chopping and seeding the pepper. When you're finished, wash your hands thoroughly in hot soapy water.

NUTRITIONAL VALUES PER APPETIZER

Calories	59	Sodium	142mg
Total Fat	2g	Total Carbohydrate	8g
Saturated Fat	1g	Protein	2g
Cholesterol	4mg		

Chicken Broccoli Pockets

1 can (10¾ ounces) CAMPBELL'S HEALTHY REQUEST Condensed
  Cream of Chicken Soup
¼ cup water
1 tablespoon lemon juice
¼ teaspoon garlic powder
⅛ teaspoon pepper
1 cup cooked broccoli flowerets
1 medium carrot, shredded (about ½ cup)
2 cups cubed cooked chicken
3 pita breads (6-inch), cut in half, each forming 2 pockets
  Quartered cherry tomatoes for garnish
  Fresh parsley for garnish

In medium saucepan mix soup, water, lemon juice, garlic powder, pepper,
broccoli, carrot and chicken. Over medium heat, heat through. Spoon
½ cup chicken mixture into each pita half. Garnish with tomatoes and
fresh parsley. Makes 6 sandwiches.

When you need cooked chicken for a recipe, microwave or poach skinless, boneless chicken
breast halves. 12 ounces will yield 2 cups cubed cooked chicken. Or, if you like, substitute
2 cans (5 ounces each) Swanson® Premium Chunk Chicken Breast, drained.

NUTRITIONAL VALUES PER SANDWICH

Calories	202	Sodium	404mg
Total Fat	4g	Total Carbohydrate	24g
Saturated Fat	1g	Protein	16g
Cholesterol	39mg		

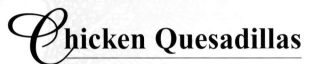hicken Quesadillas

1 can (10¾ ounces) CAMPBELL'S HEALTHY REQUEST Condensed
    Cream of Chicken Soup
1 teaspoon chili powder
½ cup shredded Cheddar cheese (2 ounces)
2 cans (5 ounces *each*) SWANSON Premium Chunk Chicken Breast *or*
    Chunk Chicken, drained
8 flour tortillas (8-inch)

1. Mix soup, chili powder, cheese and chicken.

2. Place tortillas on 2 baking sheets. Top half of each tortilla with about ¼ cup soup mixture. Spread to within ½ inch of edge. Moisten edges of tortillas with water. Fold over and press edges together.

3. Bake at 400°F. for 10 minutes or until hot. Serves 8.

These Mexican-inspired snacks double as an appetizer or as a complete meal, when teamed with soup, vegetables or salad.

NUTRITIONAL VALUES PER SERVING

Calories	199	Sodium	464mg
Total Fat	6g	Total Carbohydrate	23g
Saturated Fat	2g	Protein	12g
Cholesterol	23mg		

arbecued Turkey Pockets

1 can (10¾ ounces) CAMPBELL'S HEALTHY REQUEST Condensed
   Tomato Soup
¼ cup water
2 tablespoons packed brown sugar
2 tablespoons vinegar
1 tablespoon Worcestershire sauce
1 pound thinly sliced cooked turkey breast
3 pita breads (6-inch), cut in half, each forming 2 pockets

1. In medium skillet mix soup, water, sugar, vinegar and Worcestershire.
   Over medium heat, heat to a boil. Reduce heat to low and cook 5 minutes.

2. Add turkey and heat through. Spoon ½ cup turkey mixture into each pita
   half. Makes 6 sandwiches.

*If you don't have cooked turkey or leftover roast turkey on hand for these quick-to-fix
pockets, stop by the deli and pick up some sliced turkey breast.*

NUTRITIONAL VALUES PER SANDWICH

Calories	241	Sodium	433mg
Total Fat	2g	Total Carbohydrate	29g
Saturated Fat	0g	Protein	26g
Cholesterol	63mg		

S n a c k s   &   S a n d w i c h e s

$\mathcal{S}$ouperburgers

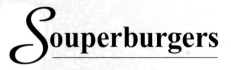

¾ **pound lean ground beef (85% lean)**
1 **medium onion, chopped (about ½ cup)**
1 **can (10¾ ounces) CAMPBELL'S HEALTHY REQUEST Condensed**
    Cream of Celery Soup
¼ **cup water**
1 **tablespoon ketchup**
⅛ **teaspoon pepper**
6 **hamburger rolls, split and toasted**

1. In medium skillet over medium-high heat, cook beef and onion until beef is browned, stirring to separate meat. Pour off fat.

2. Add soup, water, ketchup and pepper. Reduce heat to low and heat through. Divide meat mixture among rolls. Makes 6 sandwiches.

Be sure to choose 85% lean ground beef and team this recipe with fresh vegetables and a salad tossed with fat-free dressing for a well-rounded, healthful meal.

NUTRITIONAL VALUES PER SANDWICH

Calories	279	Sodium	506mg
Total Fat	11g	Total Carbohydrate	28g
Saturated Fat	4g	Protein	16g
Cholesterol	45mg		

Prep Time: 5 minutes   **Cook Time: 15 minutes**

Lite & Creamy Green Beans

1 can (10¾ ounces) **CAMPBELL'S HEALTHY REQUEST** Condensed
    Cream of Mushroom Soup
¼ cup milk
1 teaspoon soy sauce
⅛ teaspoon garlic powder
    Generous dash pepper
3 cups frozen cut green beans
2 tablespoons toasted sliced almonds for garnish

1. In medium saucepan mix soup, milk, soy, garlic powder, pepper and beans. Over medium heat, heat to a boil.

2. Reduce heat to low. Cover and cook 10 minutes or until beans are tender, stirring occasionally. Garnish with almonds. Serves 6.

Although nuts are high in fat and calories, sprinkling a few over a dish won't harm your diet. Toasting enhances their flavor, allowing you to use even fewer. To toast nuts, place in a shallow baking pan and bake at 400°F. for 7 to 8 minutes or until light brown.

NUTRITIONAL VALUES PER SERVING

Calories	62	Sodium	261mg
Total Fat	2g	Total Carbohydrate	10g
Saturated Fat	1g	Protein	2g
Cholesterol	1mg		

Roast Turkey Dinner

- Roast turkey breast
- Fat-free turkey gravy
- *Lite & Creamy Green Beans*
- Whole-grain dinner roll with 1 teaspoon margarine
- Angel food cake with fresh berries

Prep Time: 5 minutes   **Cook Time: 5 minutes**
Stand Time: 10 minutes

Creamy Souper Rice

**1 can (10¾ ounces) CAMPBELL'S HEALTHY REQUEST Condensed
    Cream of Mushroom Soup**
1½ cups water
1½ cups uncooked instant rice

1. In medium saucepan mix soup and water. Over medium-high heat, heat to a boil.

2. Stir in rice. Cover and remove from heat. Let stand 10 minutes. Fluff with fork. Serves 4.

*Keep this creamy rice dish in mind to serve with any meat, fish
or poultry. To add a little color, toss some snipped
fresh parsley with the rice.*

NUTRITIONAL VALUES PER SERVING

Calories	172	Sodium	298mg
Total Fat	1g	Total Carbohydrate	36g
Saturated Fat	1g	Protein	3g
Cholesterol	0mg		

lazed Snow Peas & Carrots

4 teaspoons cornstarch
1 can (16 ounces) CAMPBELL'S HEALTHY REQUEST Ready to
    Serve Chicken Broth
1 teaspoon lemon juice
4 medium carrots, sliced (about 2 cups)
1 medium red *or* yellow onion, coarsely chopped
    (about ½ cup)
8 ounces snow peas (about 2 cups)
    Lemon wedges for garnish

1. In cup mix cornstarch, *½ cup* broth and lemon juice until smooth.
   Set aside.

2. In medium skillet mix remaining broth, carrots and onion. Over high
   heat, heat to a boil. Reduce heat to medium. Cover and cook 5 minutes
   or until vegetables are tender. Add snow peas. Cook 2 minutes.

3. Stir cornstarch mixture and add. Cook until mixture boils and thickens,
   stirring constantly. Garnish with lemon wedges. Serves 6.

*With their fresh, slightly sweet flavor and crisp texture, snow peas can be just the thing to
wake up tired meals. When buying snow peas, choose crisp, bright green pods that are
small and flat with immature seeds. Avoid broken,
shriveled or spotted pods.*

NUTRITIONAL VALUES PER SERVING

Calories	53	Sodium	164mg
Total Fat	0g	Total Carbohydrate	10g
Saturated Fat	0g	Protein	3g
Cholesterol	0mg		

O n   t h e   S i d e

Simply Delicious Vegetables

1 can (16 ounces) CAMPBELL'S HEALTHY REQUEST Ready to Serve Chicken Broth
1 cup broccoli flowerets
1 cup cauliflower flowerets
1 medium carrot, sliced (about ½ cup)
1 stalk celery, sliced (about ½ cup)

1. In medium saucepan mix broth, broccoli, cauliflower, carrot and celery. Over high heat, heat to a boil.

2. Reduce heat to low. Cover and cook 5 minutes or until vegetables are tender-crisp. Drain. Serves 6.

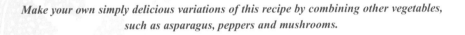

Make your own simply delicious variations of this recipe by combining other vegetables, such as asparagus, peppers and mushrooms.

NUTRITIONAL VALUES PER SERVING

Calories	20	Sodium	169mg
Total Fat	0g	Total Carbohydrate	3g
Saturated Fat	0g	Protein	2g
Cholesterol	0mg		

O n   t h e   S i d e

Broccoli Cheese Potato Topper

1 can (10¾ ounces) CAMPBELL'S HEALTHY REQUEST Condensed
    Cream of Broccoli Soup
¼ cup milk
    Dash pepper
4 large hot baked potatoes, split
1 cup cooked broccoli flowerets
¼ cup shredded Cheddar cheese (1 ounce)

1. In small bowl mix soup, milk and pepper.

2. Place hot potatoes on microwave-safe plate. Carefully fluff up potatoes with fork.

3. Top each potato with broccoli. Spoon soup mixture over potatoes. Top with cheese. Microwave on HIGH 4 minutes or until hot. Serves 4.

The choice is yours. Bake the potatoes at 400° F. for 60 minutes or microwave them on HIGH for 10½ to 12½ minutes or until fork-tender. Be sure to prick the potatoes several times with a fork before cooking.

NUTRITIONAL VALUES PER SERVING

Calories	310	Sodium	373mg
Total Fat	4g	Total Carbohydrate	59g
Saturated Fat	2g	Protein	9g
Cholesterol	12mg		

O n   t h e   S i d e

Prep Time: 5 minutes   Cook Time: 15 minutes

Easy Vegetable Combo

**1 can (10¾ ounces) CAMPBELL'S HEALTHY REQUEST Condensed
  Cream of Celery Soup**
½ cup milk
2 teaspoons lemon juice
⅛ teaspoon pepper
**1 bag (16 ounces) frozen vegetable combination (broccoli,
  cauliflower, carrots)**

1. In medium saucepan mix soup, milk, lemon juice, pepper and vegetables.
   Over medium heat, heat to a boil.

2. Reduce heat to low. Cover and cook 10 minutes or until vegetables are
   tender, stirring occasionally. Serves 6.

*A healthy eating plan includes three to five servings of vegetables each day. Select a wide
variety of both dark green and leafy vegetables, such as spinach, broccoli and cabbage; and
deep yellow and orange ones, such as carrots, sweet potatoes
and acorn squash.*

NUTRITIONAL VALUES PER SERVING

Calories	62	Sodium	234mg
Total Fat	1g	Total Carbohydrate	10g
Saturated Fat	0g	Protein	3g
Cholesterol	4mg		

O n   t h e   S i d e

Tomato-Basil Zucchini

1 can (10¾ ounces) CAMPBELL'S HEALTHY REQUEST Condensed
   Tomato Soup
2 tablespoons grated Parmesan cheese
1 tablespoon lemon juice
½ teaspoon dried basil leaves, crushed
½ teaspoon garlic powder
4 medium zucchini, sliced (about 6 cups)
1 small green pepper, cut into 2-inch-long strips (about 1 cup)
1 large onion, sliced (about 1 cup)
   Fresh basil for garnish

1. In Dutch oven mix soup, cheese, lemon juice, basil, garlic powder,
   zucchini, pepper and onion. Over medium heat, heat to a boil.

2. Reduce heat to low. Cover and cook 15 minutes or until vegetables are
   tender, stirring often. Garnish with fresh basil. Serves 8.

Delicious any time of the year, this side dish is at its best in the summer when zucchini is
plentiful. Tote it to a potluck supper or a family reunion. Serve it with soup and fresh fruit
for a quick and breezy meal.

NUTRITIONAL VALUES PER SERVING

Calories	59	Sodium	172mg
Total Fat	1g	Total Carbohydrate	11g
Saturated Fat	0g	Protein	3g
Cholesterol	1mg		

Vegetable Rice Pilaf

Vegetable cooking spray
¼ **cup chopped green** *or* **red pepper**
2 **cloves garlic, minced**
½ **teaspoon dried basil leaves, crushed**
⅛ **teaspoon black pepper**
1 **cup uncooked regular long-grain white rice**
1 **can (16 ounces) CAMPBELL'S HEALTHY REQUEST Ready to Serve Chicken Broth**
¾ **cup frozen mixed vegetables**

1. Spray medium skillet with cooking spray and heat over medium heat 1 minute. Add green pepper, garlic, basil, black pepper and rice. Cook until rice is browned and green pepper is tender and crisp, stirring constantly.

2. Stir in broth. Heat to a boil. Reduce heat to low. Cover and cook 10 minutes.

3. Stir in vegetables. Cover and cook 10 minutes more or until rice is done and most of liquid is absorbed Serves 4.

Try this delicious rice side dish as a healthier alternative to packaged rice mixes. Rice is an excellent source of complex carbohydrates, as well as calcium, iron and B vitamins.

NUTRITIONAL VALUES PER SERVING

Calories	204	Sodium	241mg
Total Fat	1g	Total Carbohydrate	43g
Saturated Fat	0g	Protein	6g
Cholesterol	0mg		

Index

WEIGHTS AND MEASURES

3 teaspoons.................1 tablespoon		2 cups.........................1 pint	
4 tablespoons.............¼ cup		4 cups.........................1 quart	
5⅓ tablespoons.............⅓ cup		2 pints.........................1 quart	
8 tablespoons.............½ cup		4 quarts.........................1 gallon	
10⅔ tablespoons.............⅔ cup		1 tablespoon................½ fluid ounce	
12 tablespoons.............¾ cup		1 cup...........................8 fluid ounces	
16 tablespoons.............1 cup		1 cup...........................½ pint	

Preparation and Cooking Times: Every recipe was developed and tested in Campbell's Global Consumer Food Center by professional home economists. Use "Prep Time," "Cook Time" and/or "Stand Time" given with each recipe as guides. The preparation times are based on the approximate amount of time required to assemble the recipes before baking or cooking. These times include preparation steps, such as chopping, mixing, cooking rice, pasta, vegetables, etc. The fact that some preparation steps can be done simultaneously or during cooking is taken into account. The cook times are based on the minimum amount of time required to cook, bake or broil the food in the recipes.

Recipe and Nutrition Values: Values are approximate; calculations are based upon food composition data in the Campbell Soup Company Master Data Base. Some variation in nutrition values may result from periodic product changes.

Calculation of Nutritional Information: When a choice is given for an ingredient, calculations are based upon the first choice listed. Garnishes and optional ingredients are not included in the calculations. The following information is provided for each recipe serving: calories, total fat, saturated fat, cholesterol and sodium in milligrams (mg); and total carbohydrate and protein in grams (g).

Campbell's® Healthy Request™ *Healthy Cooking Made Easy* was developed by Campbell Soup Company, Campbell Place, Camden, NJ 08103-1799. For more delicious Campbell's® Healthy Request® recipes and other great ideas, visit our Web site at: www.healthyrequest.com

Published by Meredith Custom Publishing, 1912 Grand Avenue, Des Moines, IA 50309-3379.
Printed in Hong Kong. Canadian BN 12348 2887 RT.

Metric Chart

Metric Cooking Hints

By making a few conversions, cooks in Australia, Canada, and the United Kingdom can use the recipes in *Campbell's® Healthy Request™ Healthy Cooking Made Easy* with confidence. The charts on this page provide a guide for converting measurements from the U.S. customary system, which is used throughout this book, to the imperial and metric systems. There also is a conversion table for oven temperatures to accommodate the differences in oven calibrations.

Product Differences: Most of the ingredients called for in the recipes in this book are available in English-speaking countries. However, some are known by different names. Here are some common American ingredients and their possible counterparts:

- Sugar is granulated or castor sugar.
- Powdered sugar is icing sugar.
- All-purpose flour is plain household flour or white flour. When self-rising flour is used in place of all-purpose flour in a recipe that calls for leavening, omit the leavening agent (baking soda or baking powder) and salt.
- Light-colored corn syrup is golden syrup.
- Cornstarch is cornflour.
- Baking soda is bicarbonate of soda.
- Vanilla is vanilla essence.
- Green, red or yellow sweet peppers are capsicums.
- Golden raisins are sultanas.

Volume and Weight: Americans traditionally use cup measures for liquid and solid ingredients. The chart, above right, shows the approximate imperial and metric equivalents. If you are accustomed to weighing solid ingredients, the following approximate equivalents will be helpful.

- 1 cup butter, castor sugar, or rice = 8 ounces = about 250 grams
- 1 cup flour = 4 ounces = about 125 grams
- 1 cup icing sugar = 5 ounces = about 150 grams

   Spoon measures are used for smaller amounts of ingredients. Although the size of the tablespoon varies slightly in different countries, for practical purposes and for recipes in this book, a straight substitution is all that's necessary.

   Measurements made using cups or spoons always should be level unless stated otherwise.

Equivalents: U.S. = Australia/U.K.

⅛ teaspoon = 0.5 ml	¾ cup = ⅔ cup = 6 fluid ounces = 180 ml
¼ teaspoon = 1 ml	1 cup = ¾ cup = 8 fluid ounces = 240 ml
½ teaspoon = 2 ml	1¼ cups = 1 cup
1 teaspoon = 5 ml	2 cups = 1 pint
1 tablespoon = 1 tablespoon	1 quart = 1 litre
¼ cup = 2 tablespoons = 2 fluid ounces = 60 ml	½ inch =1.27 cm
⅓ cup = ¼ cup = 3 fluid ounces = 90 ml	1 inch = 2.54 cm
½ cup = ⅓ cup = 4 fluid ounces = 120 ml	
⅔ cup = ½ cup = 5 fluid ounces = 150 ml	

Baking Pan Sizes

American	Metric
8x1½-inch round baking pan	20x4-centimetre cake tin
9x1½-inch round baking pan	23x3.5-centimetre cake tin
11x7x1½-inch baking pan	28x18x4-centimetre baking tin
13x9x2-inch baking pan	30x20x3-centimetre baking tin
2-quart rectangular baking dish	30x20x3-centimetre baking tin
15x10x1-inch baking pan	30x25x2-centimetre baking tin (Swiss roll tin)
9-inch pie plate	22x4- or 23x4-centimetre pie plate
7- or 8-inch springform pan	18- or 20-centimetre springform or loose-bottom cake tin
9x5x3-inch loaf pan	23x13x7-centimetre or 2-pound narrow loaf tin or paté tin
1½-quart casserole	1.5-litre casserole
2-quart casserole	2-litre casserole

Oven Temperature Equivalents

Fahrenheit Setting	Celsius Setting*	Gas Setting
300°F	150°C	Gas Mark 2 (slow)
325°F	160°C	Gas Mark 3 (moderately slow)
350°F	180°C	Gas Mark 4 (moderate)
375°F	190°C	Gas Mark 5 (moderately hot)
400°F	200°C	Gas Mark 6 (hot)
425°F	220°C	Gas Mark 7
450°F	230°C	Gas Mark 8 (very hot)
Broil		Grill

* Electric and gas ovens may be calibrated using Celsius. However, for an electric oven, increase the Celsius setting 10 to 20 degrees when cooking above 160°C. For convection or forced-air ovens (gas or electric), lower the temperature setting 10°C when cooking at all heat levels.